LEVEL
1

T. rex

Andrea Silen

Washington, D.C.

For Owen —A.S.

Published by National Geographic Partners, LLC, Washington, DC 20036.

Designed by Gus Tello

Library of Congress Cataloging-in-Publication Data

Names: Silen, Andrea, author.
Title: T. rex / Andrea Silen.
Description: Washington, D.C. : National Geographic, 2022. | Series: National Geographic readers | Audience: Ages 4-6 | Audience: Grades K-1
Identifiers: LCCN 2021019585 (print) | LCCN 2021019586 (ebook) | ISBN 9781426372735 (paperback) | ISBN 9781426373015 (library binding) | ISBN 9781426373138 (ebook)
Subjects: LCSH: Tyrannosaurus rex--Juvenile literature.
Classification: LCC QE862.S3 S4826 2022 (print) | LCC QE862.S3 (ebook) | DDC 567.912/9--dc23
LC record available at https://lccn.loc.gov/2021019585
LC ebook record available at https://lccn.loc.gov/2021019586

The author and publisher gratefully acknowledge the expert content review of this book by Nizar Ibrahim, Ph.D., University of Portsmouth (U.K.) and University of Detroit Mercy (U.S.A.), anatomist, paleobiologist, and National Geographic Explorer, as well as the literacy review of this book by Mariam Jean Dreher, professor emerita of reading education, University of Maryland, College Park.

Photo Credits

Cover, Franco Tempesta/National Geographic Partners, LLC; 1, Franco Tempesta; 3, Mohamad Haghani/Stocktrek Images/Getty Images; 4-5 (header throughout), pandavector/Adobe Stock; 4-5, Warpaint/Shutterstock; 6 (UP), matis75/Adobe Stock; 6 (LO), Herschel Hoffmeyer/Shutterstock; 7, Orlando Florin Rosu/Adobe Stock; 8-9, matis75/Adobe Stock; 10, Mohamad Haghani/Stocktrek Images/Getty Images; 11, Kurt Miller/Stocktrek Images/Getty Images; 11 (icon throughout), Serhii/Adobe Stock; 12-13, Franco Tempesta/National Geographic Partners, LLC; 14, YuRi Photolife/Shutterstock; 15, Franco Tempesta/National Geographic Partners, LLC; 16-17, Jerry LoFaro/Stocktrek Images/Alamy Stock Photo; 18 (UP), Herschel Hoffmeyer/Shutterstock; 18 (CTR), Marques/Shutterstock; 18 (LO), Donna Ikenberry/Art Directors/Alamy Stock Photo; 19 (UP LE), Leonello Calvetti/Stocktrek Images/Getty Images; 19 (UP RT), Jerry LoFaro/Stocktrek Images/Alamy Stock Photo; 19 (LO), Daniel/Adobe Stock; 20, courtesy Museum of the Rockies; 21, Corbin17/Alamy Stock Photo; 22, Amanda Kelley; 23, Cuson/Shutterstock; 24 (LE), David Davis Photoproductions/Alamy Stock Photo; 24 (RT), Dirk Lammers/AP/Shutterstock; 25, schusterbauer/Adobe Stock; 26-27, Amanda Kelley; 28, Franco Tempesta; 29 (LE), stevew_photo/Adobe Stock; 29 (RT), sergei_fish13/Adobe Stock; 30 (LE), blickwinkel/Alamy Stock Photo; 30 (RT), lpictures/Adobe Stock; 31 (UP LE), Alex Ramsay/Alamy Stock Photo; 31 (UP RT), Corbin17/Alamy Stock Photo; 31 (LO RT), TTstudio/Adobe Stock; 31 (LO LE), YuRi Photolife/Shutterstock; 32 (UP), metha1819/Shutterstock; 32 (UP LE), National Geographic Partners, LLC; 32 (CTR RT), Pao W/Shutterstock; 32 (LO LE), courtesy Museum of the Rockies; 32 (LO RT), lpictures/Adobe Stock

Printed in the United States of America
22/WOR/1

Contents

T. rex Rules!

T. rex was one of the most powerful dinosaurs on Earth.

You would not want to mess with *Tyrannosaurus rex* (Tye-RAN-oh-SORE-us REX).

T. rex had big teeth. It had sharp claws. And it was as long as a bus. Yikes! Let's meet this big, fierce (FEERSS) dinosaur.

Where T. rex Lived

T. rex walked on Earth millions of years ago. It lived in parts of North America.

Some scientists (SYE-un-tists) think these dinosaurs lived alone. Others think they may have lived and hunted in groups.

T. rex lived in areas such as present-day Montana and Wyoming, U.S.A.

Hunting in groups would have made it easier to catch a meal.

T. rex Parts

This dinosaur's body was strong and deadly.

Each foot was longer than a tennis racket. *T. rex* walked on its toes.

T. rex's eyes worked really well. They helped the dinosaur find animals to eat.

Each arm had two fingers with claws on the ends. Each claw was about the length of a soda can.

Its teeth were the size of bananas. They could break bones in half.

The dinosaur's jaws were super strong. Its bite could have crushed a car.

Time for Dinner

T. rex was a carnivore (CAR-nuh-vore) It ate other animals. *T. rex* was fierce, but not fast. It probably couldn't catch speedy animals.

T. rex may have tried—but failed—to grab fast dinosaurs like these *Struthiomimus* (Strooth-ee-oh-MY-muss).

Slow *Edmontosaurus* (Ed-MON-toe-SORE-us) was a likely meal for *T. rex*.

T. rex Talk

CARNIVORE: An animal that eats meat

But it could catch slower plant-eating dinosaurs. Once it did, its huge jaws opened wide. Then its big teeth chomped down on its meal.

T. rex used its
sharp teeth to rip
off chunks of meat.

Scientists think *T. rex* sometimes tossed the meat into the air. Then it would catch the meat in its mouth and swallow it whole.

T. rex hunted live animals. But, like most predators today, it also ate dead animals it found.

T. rex Tots

Like other dinosaurs, *T. rex* moms laid eggs. Scientists think the eggs might have taken months to hatch. *T. rex* parents may have guarded their eggs to keep them safe.

T. rex egg fossils have not been found yet. But baby *T. rex* might have hatched from eggs that looked like this.

Scientists think *T. rex* moms could have laid about 20 eggs at one time!

A young *T. rex* grew fast. It may have gained more than four pounds a day over many years.

When the babies hatched, they were the size of small turkeys. They likely had a fluffy, feather-like covering on parts of their bodies.

As they grew, they may have lost this downy covering. Scientists don't know if the adults had feathers.

17

6 COOL THINGS
About *T. rex*

1

T. rex could eat **500 pounds** of meat in **one bite.**

2

New research suggests that **a young *T. rex*** likely had **a stronger bite** than an adult **lion or tiger.**

3

Rare footprints, likely from *T. rex,* have been **discovered** in Montana and New Mexico, U.S.A.

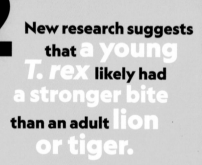

Tyrann—aurus Track

La pisada de un Tyrannosaurus

This is a —t made by a *Tyrannosaurus rex* found i— —a very end of the Cretaceous (about 66 milli— —e of shape of the track match the foot structure. —fossil track was found on the Philmont S— —onstern New Mexico near Raton.

Este es el molde de una pisada gigante hecha por un *Tyrannosaurus rex,* trallada en rocas que datan del final del período Cretácico (hace unos 66 millones de años), el tamaño y la forma de la pisada asemejan la estructura de la estructura de la pata del *T. rex.* La pisada del fósil original fue encontrada en el Rancho Philmont Boy Scout al noreste de Nuevo México, cerca de Ratón.

Touch the track and compare it to Stan's foot!

¡Toca la pisada y compárala con la pata de Stan!

4

T. rex **had about 50 to 60 teeth.**

It snacked on other dinosaurs like ***Triceratops*** **(Tri-SAIR-uh-tops).**

5

6

T. rex **probably didn't roar** like in the **movies.** Instead, it may have **hissed** like an alligator, or even **hooted like a bird!**

Finding T. rex

T. rex has been extinct (ik-STINKED) for a long time. We know about the dinosaur from fossils. Some fossils are bones. They are buried in rock. Scientists dig them up.

This *T. rex* fossil was found near Fort Peck Reservoir in Montana, U.S.A.

T. rex Talk

EXTINCT: No longer alive. When all members of an animal species are dead, the species is extinct.

FOSSIL: Parts or traces of a living thing that have been preserved in rock

a *T. rex* fossil on display at a museum

The bones can tell scientists about *T. rex*'s shape and size. They can also tell how *T. rex* lived and died.

Other fossils show *T. rex* skin. The skin left prints in mud. The mud hardened into rock to make fossils. The fossils show that adult *T. rex* likely had pebbly scales on many parts of its body.

A model of *T. rex* shows what scales on its skin probably looked like.

T. rex Talk

SCALES: Small, hard plates of skin that overlap

Meet Sue and Scotty

Scientists have dug up about 50 different *T. rex* skeletons. Many are missing a lot of bones. The most complete skeleton was found in South Dakota, U.S.A.

a close-up of Sue's head

The skeleton nicknamed Sue is at the Field Museum in Chicago, Illinois, U.S.A.

Sue is the most complete *T. rex* fossil ever found. Only a few bones are missing.

It was nicknamed Sue. Sue is as long as a bus! It is one of the largest *T. rex* skeletons.

Scotty is on display at the Royal Saskatchewan Museum in Saskatchewan, Canada.

Another very large skeleton was found in Canada. Scientists think the dinosaur weighed as much as 19,500 pounds.

They nicknamed the skeleton Scotty.

Experts also believe Scotty lived more than 30 years. That likely makes Scotty one of the oldest *T. rex* ever found.

All in the
Family

T. rex may be extinct. But it has living relatives. Birds like chickens and ostriches (OS-trich-iz) are related to *T. rex*. That means you can see some of *T. rex*'s family members today!

Today's birds are living dinosaurs!

In some ways, an ostrich skeleton looks similar to a *T. rex* skeleton.

29

What in the World?

These pictures are up-close views of things from a *T. rex*'s world. Use the hints to figure out what's in the pictures. Answers are on page 31.

1

HINT: These *T. rex* body parts were the size of bananas.

2

HINT: *T. rex* had these plates of skin.

Word Bank

Fossils   Toes   Teeth   Chicken   Eggs   Scales

3

HINT: *T. rex* walked on these.

4

HINT: We know about *T. rex* from these.

5

HINT: *T. rex* moms laid these.

6

HINT: This bird is related to *T. rex*.

GLOSSARY

CARNIVORE: An animal that eats meat

EXTINCT: No longer alive. When all members of an animal species are dead, the species is extinct.

FOSSIL: Parts or traces of a living thing that have been preserved in rock

SCALES: Small, hard plates of skin that overlap